The Wood

or

In Every Leaf

Chris White and Hannah Khalil

methuen | drama

LONDON · NEW YORK · OXFORD · NEW DELHI · SYDNEY

METHUEN DRAMA
Bloomsbury Publishing Plc
50 Bedford Square, London, WC1B 3DP, UK
1385 Broadway, New York, NY 10018, USA
29 Earlsfort Terrace, Dublin 2, Ireland

BLOOMSBURY, METHUEN DRAMA and the Methuen
Drama logo are trademarks of Bloomsbury Publishing Plc

First published in Great Britain 2023

A catalogue record for this book is available from the British Library.

A catalog record for this book is available from the Library of Congress.

ISBN: PB: 978-1-3504-4079-1
ePDF: 978-1-3504-4080-7
eBook: 978-1-3504-4081-4

Series: Plays for Young People

Typeset by Mark Heslington Ltd, Scarborough, North Yorkshire

To find out more about our authors and books visit
www.bloomsbury.com and sign up for our newsletters.

ABOUT THE ROYAL SHAKESPEARE COMPANY

The Shakespeare Memorial Theatre was founded by Charles Flower, a local brewer, and opened in Stratford-upon-Avon in 1879. Since then, the plays of Shakespeare have been performed here, alongside the work of his contemporaries and of living contemporary playwrights. In 1960, the Royal Shakespeare Company as we now know it was formed by Peter Hall and Fordham Flower. The founding principles of the Company were threefold: the Company would embrace the freedom and power of Shakespeare's work, train and develop young actors and directors and, crucially, experiment in new ways of making theatre. The RSC quickly became known for exhilarating performances of Shakespeare alongside new masterpieces such as *The Homecoming* and *Old Times* by Harold Pinter. It was a combination that thrilled audiences, and this close and exacting relationship between writers from different eras has become the fuel that powers the creativity of the RSC.

In 1974, The Other Place opened in a tin hut on Waterside under the visionary leadership and artistic directorship of Buzz Goodbody. Determined to explore Shakespeare's plays in intimate proximity to her audience and to make small-scale, radical new work, Buzz revitalised the Company's interrogation of the relationship between the contemporary and classical repertoire. This was followed by the founding of the Swan Theatre in 1986 - a space dedicated to Shakespeare's contemporaries, as well as later plays from the Restoration period, alongside living writers.

In nearly 60 years of producing new plays, we have collaborated with some of the most exciting writers of their generation. These have included: Edward Albee, Howard Barker, Alice Birch, Richard Bean, Edward Bond, Howard Brenton, Marina Carr, Lolita Chakrabarti, Caryl Churchill, Martin Crimp, Can Dündar, David Edgar, Helen Edmundson, James Fenton, Georgia Fitch, Robin French, Juliet Gilkes Romero, Fraser Grace, David Greig, Tanika Gupta, Matt Hartley, Ella Hickson, Kirsty Housley, Dennis Kelly, Hannah Khalil, Anders Lustgarten, Tarell Alvin McCraney, Martin McDonagh, Tom Morton-Smith, Rona Munro, Richard Nelson, Anthony Neilson, Harold Pinter, Phil Porter, Mike Poulton, Mark Ravenhill, Somalia Seaton, Adriano Shaplin, Tom Stoppard, debbie tucker green, Frances Ya-Chu Cowhig, Timberlake Wertenbaker, Peter Whelan and Roy Williams.

The RSC is committed to illuminating the relevance of Shakespeare's plays and the works of his contemporaries for the next generation of audiences and believes that our continued investment in new plays and living writers is a central part of that mission.

The work of the RSC is supported by the Culture Recovery Fund

New Work at the RSC is generously supported by The Drue and H.J. Heinz II Charitable Trust

The work of the RSC Learning and National Partnerships department is generously supported by Paul Hamlyn Foundation, Esmée Fairbairn Foundation, The Clore Duffield Foundation, The 29th May 1961 Charitable Trust, GRoW @ Annenberg, The Polonsky Foundation, Stratford Town Trust, LSEG Foundation, The Goldsmiths' Company Charity, HDH Wills 1965 Charitable Trust, Teale Charitable Trust, The Grimmitt Trust, The Oakley Charitable Trust, and Misses Barrie Charitable Trust

Supported using public funding by
**ARTS COUNCIL
ENGLAND**

NEW WORK AT THE RSC

We are a contemporary theatre company built on classical rigour. Through an extensive programme of research and development, we resource writers, directors and actors to explore and develop new ideas for our stages, and as part of this we commission playwrights to engage with the muscularity and ambition of the classics and to set Shakespeare's world in the context of our own.

We invite writers to spend time with us in our rehearsal rooms, with our actors and creative teams. Alongside developing new plays for all our stages, we invite playwrights to contribute dramaturgically to both our productions of Shakespeare and his contemporaries, as well as our work for, and with, young people. We believe that engaging with living writers and contemporary theatre-makers helps to establish a creative culture within the Company which both inspires new work and creates an ever more urgent sense of enquiry into the classics.

Shakespeare was a great innovator and breaker of rules, as well as a bold commentator on the times in which he lived. It is his spirit which informs new work at the RSC.

Support us and make a difference
For more information visit **www.rsc.org.uk/support**

RSC NATIONAL AND STRATFORD PLAYMAKING FESTIVALS

***The Wood of Words* or *In Every Leaf* was first presented as part of the Royal Shakespeare Company's National and Stratford Playmaking Festivals in July 2023.**

The casts consisted of over 300 young people, led by their teachers from schools across the country and Stratford-upon-Avon who work in partnership with the RSC and regional theatres through the Associate Schools Programme.

The Associate Schools Programme is the Royal Shakespeare Company's Partnership programme with Regional Theatres and schools across England. Through the programme, schools form and work in local partnerships to develop communities of practice and research inspired by Shakespeare's work. The programme aims to enrich the teaching, learning and enjoyment of Shakespeare's work across the country.

Playmaking is part of an annual celebration, involving thousands of young people across the country performing Shakespeare's plays in Regional Theatres, schools, community venues and in Stratford-upon-Avon. Performances are created in collaboration with young people, teachers, RSC artists and theatre makers.

The Wood of Words or *In Every Leaf* was first presented as part of the Royal Shakespeare Company's National and Stratford Playmaking Festivals at the Royal Shakespeare Theatre, Stratford-upon-Avon, on 11 July and 14 July 2023.

CHAPTER 1

Featuring young people from across Leamington Spa for the National Playmaking Festival:

ALFIE
AYLA
CHLOE
CLARA
EVIE
GEORGE
IONA
JACY
JAMES
JEAN
KELSIE
KYMRHON
LEON
MACIE
MARIA
OTTO
SEBASTIAN
SIMRAN
STANLEY
WILLOW

Led by teachers:
DEBBIE HILL
ROH KEYS
PAIGE MURPHY

Featuring students from Bishopton Primary School, Stratford-upon-Avon for the Stratford Playmaking Festival:

ALICE
AMELIA
CHARLOTTE
ETHAN
GABE
HADRIEL
ISABEL
JEM
LACEY
LEANNA
MARIA
OLIVER
OLIVIA
ORE
POLINA
POPPY
RAMAZAN
SCARLETT
SHREYAN
THARUNYA
TILLIE-MAI
VIHAAN

Led by teachers:
LIZ GRAVER
VIV GRAVER

CHAPTER 2

Featuring young people from
across Birmingham for the
National Playmaking Festival:

AHMED
FATIMA
HANA
HIBBA
INSANULLAH
ISRAA
KASHAN
KENZA
LINTA
MELISSA
MERIEM
MOHAMMED
MYA
NAJAH
SAKINAH
YAEESH
YAHYA
ZAHRA
ZELLA
ZOYA

Led by teachers:
SEBRINA BLACKSTOCK MILLER
SARAH HEWITT CLARKSON
AMY LASSMAN

Featuring students from
Holy Trinity CofE Primary School,
Stratford-upon-Avon for the
Stratford Playmaking Festival:

ALESSIA
ALICE
ALYANNA
ANNA
ANNABEL
BLUEBELL
CARINA
CHARLIE
DANIEL
ELOISE
EMELIA
EMILY
GABRIELLA
HAL
JAN
LUCY B.
LUCY C.
LUNA
LUYANDA
MAX
MELEK
OLIVIA
OSKAR
POPPY
ROSE
SAM
SKYLA
SOFIA
TALLULAH

Led by teachers:
ROSE COTTRELL
JOSEPH FRERICHS

CHAPTER 3

Featuring young people across Leicester for the National Playmaking Festival:

ANUSKA
AYESHA
BETHANY
DIYA
ELSIE-MAY
EMERSON
GIRISHA
ILHAM
IMOGEN
ISAAC
LENNON
MADDISON
SAFIA
SOPHIE
THIERRY

Led by teachers:
EMILY O'FLYNN
ABI MASIH
KAT SMOCZYNSKI
ELISE WALTON

Featuring students from Stratford-upon-Avon School for the Stratford Playmaking Festival:

EDIE
ELLA
ELLA
ELLIE
FLO
HARLEY
HARRY
LEWIS
LIUBA
LIV
LIZZIE
LOUIE
MAX
MIA
NED
NIKKI
POPPY
POPPY
RUBEN
SOPHIE
TILDA

Led by teachers:
CLAIRE HOPKINS
AMY LEWIS

CHAPTER 4

Featuring young people from across Nottingham for the National Playmaking Festival:

ADAKU
ALEXA
AMBER
ARIA
ASEDA
BELLA
BRODY
CARTER
ETHAN
HECTOR
ISABELLA
ISAIAH
JAMIE
LEO
NAOMI
PEARL
REMIE
REMY
SAHARA

Led by teachers:
JOSHUA GRIMSHAW
TERESA MASON
SALLY OWENS

Featuring students from Stratford Girls' Grammar School and King Edward VI School, Stratford-upon-Avon for the Stratford Playmaking Festival:

AZ
BEA
CIARA
DEV
DYLAN
EILIS
EMMA
ESME
GRACE
JACOB
LILLY
LILY
LOUISA
OLIVIA
POPPY
RHIANNA
SOFIA
YASH

Led by teachers:
SUSAN FRATER
LOUISA NIGHTINGALE
OLIVIA SHAW
SAJ ZAIDI

CHAPTER 5

Featuring young people
from across Barking for the
National Playmaking Festival:

Featuring students from
Thomas Jolyffe Primary School,
Stratford-upon-Avon for the
Stratford Playmaking Festival:

AAILA
AMARNDAS
ANASTASIJA
ARBERESHA
CASPER
DEMARIO
ERIC
JASMINE
KAMIYA
KAREEMAH
LOLA
NAOMIE
NATHALIE
RAYHAN
RONNI
ROSIE
SHINAAYO
TANISHA
TUKUMBO
YUSUF

Led by teachers:
ANITA ARK
TOM BATES
FEHMIDA IQBAL

AVA
CHARLIE
DARCIE
DARSH
DYLAN
ELLIE
FINLEY
FLAWIA
FYNN
GENEVIEVE
HARRY
HOLLY
HUBERT
IVORY
JAMES
MARGO
MIA
MILES
MIRA
ORLA
OSCAR C
OSCAR P
SHIELA
TOBY
USMAN

Led by teacher:
BEN PHIPPS

CHAPTER 6

Featuring young people from across Bradford for the National Playmaking Festival:

BHOUTHAYNA
CALEB
COLLIN
FATOUMATA
ISAAC
JOSIAH
JOY
MARQUEZ
SAM
SAMANTHA
SARA
SCARLETT

Led by:
VANESSA ADAMS
ANGELA FISHER
CAMILLA FLETCHER
BETH LUSH
NICOLA OLDFIELD
SHARON TAYLOR

Featuring students from Bridgetown Primary School, Stratford-upon-Avon for the Stratford Playmaking Festival:

AIMEE
AMELIA
AMELIA
AMELIE
AVA
AYA
BROOKE
CHARLIE
ELIZABETH
ELLA
EMILY
FLO
GEORGIA
GRACE
ISLA
JACOB
JACOB
LILY-MAI
LOGAN
MAISIE
NITHILA
OLIVIA
OLLIE
TATIANA
THOMAS
TILLY
ZED

Led by teacher:
SARAH BILES
SALLY D'AMBROSIO
EMILY WOODCOCK

CHAPTER 7

Featuring young people
from across York for the
National Playmaking Festival:

ALEXANDER
AMELIA
BELLA
CHARLIE
ELI
ELIZABETH
ERIN
FREYA
GILDA
JULES
LILY
MATILDA
REUBEN
SAM
THEO
TOBY
TOMMY
WILLIAM

Led by teachers:
JUSTINE BURROUGHS
AMY GREENE
NICOLA TOWLE

Featuring students from
Alveston CofE Primary School,
Stratford-upon-Avon for the
Stratford Playmaking Festival:

ARLEY
ASHLEIGH
BELLA
CHLOE
ELSIE
FELIX
FLORENCE
GEORGE
GEORGIA
HANNAH
JENSON
LENNY
MATTHEW
MAX
MCKENZIE
MIA
MILLIE L
MILLIE M-W
MOLLY
NOAH
OLLIE
OSCAR E
OSCAR M
SAM
SERENA
TABITHA
THOMAS
TJ
TOM
WILLIAM

Led by teacher:
LOU CHANDLER
MRS SANDERSON

WRITTEN BY	**CHRIS WHITE & HANNAH KHALIL** **from the Works of Shakespeare**
PLAYMAKING PROJECT LEAD	**PAUL AINSWORTH**
NATIONAL FESTIVAL DIRECTOR	**CHRIS WHITE**
STRATFORD FESTIVAL DIRECTOR	**FIONA ROSS**
DESIGNER	**PIP TERRY**
COMPOSER & MUSIC DIRECTOR	**KATHERINE GILLHAM**
DIRECTOR MENTORS	**PETER BRADLEY**
	EWA DINA
	OLIVER LYNES
	JULIAN OLLIVE
	JULIA SMITH
	YASMIN TAHERI
PRODUCTION MANAGER	**DAN AVERY**
STAGE MANAGER	**JULES REED**
LEAD COORDINATOR	**ESTHER LEITH**

MUSICIANS

GUITARS	**NICK LEE**
PERCUSSION & GUITAR	**PHIL JAMES**
KEYBOARD	**BRUCE O'NEIL**

This text may differ slightly from the play as performed.

Author introduction

Early in 2023, we were approached by the Royal Shakespeare Company's Learning and National Partnerships department with an exciting proposal to make a new play from the works of Shakespeare to be presented as part of the Playmaking Festival 2023, an annual project that brings the RSC's Associate Schools to Stratford to perform a play on the main RST stage. Usually the play in question is by Shakespeare, but 2023 is special as it is the 400th anniversary of the First Folio: the first time Shakespeare's plays were gathered together and published. This happened seven years after his death and was a considerable act of friendship and dedication, by a group of his colleagues and friends, principally John Heminge and Henry Condell. Without that First Folio, many of the Bard's plays would have been lost.

So, we were tasked with making a new play which would include seven scenes from seven of Shakespeare's plays that we wouldn't know without the First Folio. We needed to dream up a concept that could bring together those scenes, and wanted to celebrate the act of friendship enacted by Shakespeare's colleagues, so held the theme of friendship close in our imaginings.

We have worked together many times as director (Chris) and writer (Hannah) but this is the first time we've created a new play on the page together. We hope you enjoy reading and performing *The Wood of Words* as much as we have enjoyed making it. We also have to thank our daughter Muna for the beautiful subtitle, 'In Every Leaf', which we love for its literary and arboreal double meaning.

Chris White and Hannah Khalil, 2023

The Wood of Words
or
In Every Leaf

Newcomers *arrive in a forest seeking refuge. There can be as few as two or as many as fourteen. We have here allocated for fourteen, but you may allocate the* **Newcomers** *to suit the number in your production. In the case that you only have two* **Newcomers** *the parts of* **Newcomers One–Twelve** *in the final scene should be read by the* **Heart of the Forest**.

At intervals pieces of paper fall from the sky like leaves from a tree. They contain messages for the young people – the **Newcomers** *to this forest. The* **Newcomers** *gather them up in one place – they will need them at the end . . . Every time a leaf falls we should hear a snippet of the music from the song of the forest.*

Before the Prologue begins we hear voices all around us that give us young people's responses to the question: 'What makes you want to run away/seek sanctuary?' . . . This crescendos until they arrive . . .

The young people – **Newcomers** *(up to fourteen) – arrive on stage; they have been seeking sanctuary and now find themselves in a forest. Throughout the play the forest throws different scenes into their path. It's like the shaking of a snow globe; they appear, then fade and then the next one comes. The* **Newcomers** *try to understand what the forest is telling them as they watch. The Shakespearean characters in the scenes do not see the* **Newcomers** *or interact with them unless otherwise specified . . . The character of the* **Heart of the Forest** *we see only once in the final scene, but they are represented throughout by the music.*

Prologue

The Newcomers' Arrival

Can be allocated in any way between the **Newcomers**.

Lonely,
apart.
My heart is heavy
As full of sorrows as the sea of sands
I should have scratched out your unseeing eyes
I'll run away till I am bigger,
but then I'll fight.

Denmark's a prison
There's no remedy
I am lost
The best is past
I needs must lose myself.

Their thoughts and whispers
The secret whispers
Snakes sting my heart!
I dare not say I have one friend alive

The more thou damm'st it up, the more it burns
I am not able to stand alone:
The world to me is a lasting storm
all hopes are lost.
I needs must lose myself.

Forspent with toil, as runners with a race,
I lay me down a little while to breathe;
I am stifled
My spirits, as in a dream, are all bound up
Even to falling
O that you bore the mind that I do.

Use your legs,
take the start,
run away.
I will not rest till I have run some ground.
I cannot cog,

I cannot prate,
I'll run from thee and hide me in the brakes.

I cannot hide
I wish mine eyes would shut up my thoughts
Hell is empty
my hopes lie drown'd,
bitter quiet
Heartsore sighs
Lonely,
apart.

All Newcomers   I will no longer endure it.

A change: they have arrived and begin to discover the woods around them.

What place is this?
Uninhabitable and almost inaccessible
How lush and lusty the grass looks
Huh?
The ground
The ground?
Has an eye of green
What time of day is it?
Time to be honest
Let's go home.
Never
I want to go home
I die for food
You shall not die for lack of dinner
But why are we here?
To be away from there
And what will we do?
Find a reason
A new space
A story!
I like this place, and would willingly waste my time in it,

A loud noise.

Chapter One

Banishment

The first story appears from As You Like It *with a cheering throng of people who rush on following a wrestling match.*

The **Newcomers** *retreat, leaving* **Newcomers One** *and* **Two** *onstage watching the wrestling with the throng.*

Newcomer One   What's happening?

Within the throng are **Rosalind**, **Celia** *and* **Duke Frederick**, *also* **Charles** *and* **Orlando** *who are wrestling.* **Rosalind** *sits silently looking desolate and sad.*

Duke Frederick (*to* **Celia** *and* **Rosalind**)
How now, daughter and cousin! Are you crept hither to
see the wrestling?
You will take little delight in it, I can tell you,
It is the first time that ever I heard breaking of ribs was
sport for ladies.

Charles
Come, where is this young gallant that is so desirous to lie
with his mother earth?

Orlando
You mean to mock me after; you should not have mock'd
me before; but come your ways.

They wrestle, **Charles** *is thrown down, cheering from the crowd.*

Duke Frederick
No more, no more.

Orlando
Yes, I beseech your Grace; I am not yet well breath'd.

Duke Frederick
Bear him away.

As **Orlando** *is dragged off the crowd follow booing.* **Charles** *and* **Duke Frederick** *follow on.*

Newcomer One   What place is this?

Newcomer Two   Where we are blown with restless violence!

Newcomer One   And why is she so sad? (*Indicating*
Rosalind.)

Newcomer Two   Shhh – watch.

Celia

Why, cousin! Why, Rosalind! Cupid have mercy, not a
word?

Rosalind

Not one to throw at a dog.

Celia

No, thy words are too precious to be cast away upon curs.
Throw some of them at me.
Come, is all this for your father?

Rosalind

No, some of it is for my child's father. O, how full of briers
is this working-day world! Look, here comes the Duke.

Celia

With his eyes full of anger.

Duke Frederick *returns with his attendants.*

Duke Frederick

Mistress, dispatch you with your safest haste,
And get you from our court.

Rosalind

Me, uncle?

Duke Frederick

You, cousin.
Within these ten days if that thou beest found
So near our public court as twenty miles,
Thou diest for it.

Rosalind
> I do beseech your Grace,
> Let me the knowledge of my fault bear with me.

Duke Frederick
> Thou art thy father's daughter. There's enough.

Rosalind
> So was I when your Highness took his dukedom.
> So was I when your Highness banished him.
> Treason is not inherited, my lord,
> And my father was no traitor.

Celia
> Dear sovereign, hear me speak.

Duke Frederick
> Ay, Celia, we stayed her for your sake;

Celia
> I was too young that time to value her,
> But now I know her. If she be a traitor,
> Why, so am I.

Duke Frederick
> She is too subtle for thee, and her smoothness,
> Her very silence, and her patience
> Speak to the people, and they pity her.
> Firm and irrevocable is my doom
> Which I have passed upon her. She is banished.

Celia
> Pronounce that sentence then on me, my liege.
> I cannot live out of her company.

Duke Frederick
> You are a fool. – You, niece, provide yourself.
> If you outstay the time, upon mine honour
> And in the greatness of my word, you die.

Duke *exits*.

A leaf of paper drops as the snippet of music plays.

Newcomer One   Strange melody.

Newcomer Two   Tongues in trees.

Newcomer One (*reading the paper*)   It says: 'Briers shall have leaves as well as thorns.'

Newcomer Two   Where will they go?

Beat.

Newcomer Two   'Briers shall have leaves as well as thorns' – what does it mean?

Newcomer One   Who knows – but I think it's important . . . Remember she said 'words are too precious to be cast away' – give it to her . . . go on!

As they try to hand the paper to **Rosalind** *who cannot see them,* **Celia** *speaks.*

Celia
O my poor Rosalind, whither wilt thou go?
I charge thee, be not thou more grieved than I am.

Rosalind
I have more cause.

Celia
Prithee, be cheerful. Know'st thou not the Duke
Hath banished me, his daughter?

Rosalind
That he hath not.

Celia
No, hath not? Rosalind lacks then the love
Which teacheth thee that thou and I am one.

Shall we be sundered? Shall we part, sweet girl?
No, let my father seek another heir.
Therefore devise with me how we may fly,
Whither to go, and what to bear with us,

Rosalind
Why, whither shall we go?

Celia
To seek your father in the Forest of Arden.

Rosalind
Alas, what danger will it be to us?

Celia
I'll put myself in poor and mean attire,
And with a kind of umber smirch my face.
The like do you. So shall we pass along
And never stir assailants. Let's away

Newcomer One   Sent her away.

Newcomer Two   She's going into the woods.

Newcomer One   Like us.

Newcomer Two   But she has no choice.

Newcomer One   Don't know if I could do that.

Newcomer Two   You did – we're here!

Newcomer One   No, I mean give up everything for a friend.

Newcomer Two   Like I said we're here aren't we?

Beat.

Newcomer One   Do you think they'll be ok those two?

They look at each other and hold hands.

Newcomer Two   I hope so.

Beat.

Newcomer One   She couldn't hear us when we talked to her . . .

Newcomer Two   It's like magic – as if someone's casting a spell for us!

Newcomer One
> If this be magic, let it be an art
> Lawful as eating.

The story moves on into . . .

Chapter Two

The Storm

A new chapter from The Tempest *swirls in as a squall of bodies rages in with* **Miranda** *and* **Prospero** *at its heart – in the eye of the storm.* **Prospero** *is in control,* **Miranda** *horrified.*

Newcomers Three *and* **Four** *watch on.*

Sailors in the Storm
> Heigh my hearts
> Yare, yare!
> Take in the topsail
> Tend to the master's whistle
> Blow
> Blow til thou burst
> Blow til thou burst thy wind

Miranda
> If by your art, my dearest father, you have
> Put the wild waters in this roar, allay them.
> The sky, it seems, would pour down stinking pitch,
> But that the sea, mounting to th' welkin's cheek,
> Dashes the fire out.

Sailors in the Storm
> I pray now
> Keep below
> Remember whom thou hast aboard
> None that I love more than myself
> Out of our way I say
> Out of our way
> Down with the topmast

Lower!
Have you a mind to sink?
A pox on your throat, you bawling, blasphemous,
uncharitable dog!

Miranda

O, I have suffered
With those that I saw suffer! A brave vessel,
Who had no doubt some noble creature in her,
Dash'd all to pieces! O, the cry did knock
Against my very heart!

Sailors in the Storm

All lost
To prayers, to prayers
All lost
We split
Mercy on us
We split

Miranda

Poor souls, they perished.
Had I been any god of power, I would
Have sunk the sea within the earth or ere
It should the good ship so have swallow'd and
The fraughting souls within her.

Prospero

Be connected;
No more amazement; tell your piteous heart
There's no harm done.

Miranda

O, woe the day!

Miranda *exits*.

Prospero

No harm. But – here's harm . . .
Thou poisonous slave, got by the devil himself
Upon thy wicked dam, come forth!

Prospero *conjures* **Caliban**.

Caliban *is formed before our very eyes – made up of several people who come together in interesting shapes to create him; perhaps by the same people who comprised the storm.*

Newcomer Three   What have we here?

Newcomer Four   A man or fish?

Newcomer Three   A strange fish.

Newcomer Four   This is no fish.

Caliban
  As wicked dew as e'er my mother brush'd
  With raven's feather from unwholesome fen
  Drop on you all! A south-west blow on ye,
  And blister you all o'er!

Prospero
  For this, be sure, tonight thou shalt have cramps,
  Side-stitches that shall pen thy breath up; urchins
  Shall forth at vast of night that they may work
  All exercise on thee. Thou shalt be pinch'd
  As thick as honeycomb, each pinch more stinging
  Than bees that made them.

Caliban
  This island's mine, by Sycorax my mother,
  Which thou tak'st from me. When thou cam'st first,
  Thou strok'st me and made much of me; wouldst give me
  Water with berries in 't; and then I lov'd thee,
  And show'd thee all the qualities o' th' isle,
  The fresh springs, brine-pits, barren place, and fertile.
  Curs'd be I that did so! All the charms
  Of Sycorax, toads, beetles, bats, light on you!
  For I am all the subjects that you have,
  Which first was mine own King; and here you sty me

Prospero
  Thou most lying slave,
  Whom stripes may move, not kindness! I have us'd thee,
  Filth as thou art, with human care, I pitied thee,

Took pains to make thee speak, taught thee each hour
One thing or other: when thou didst not, savage,
Know thine own meaning, but wouldst gabble like
A thing most brutish, I endow'd thy purposes
With words that made them known.

Caliban
You taught me language, and my profit on 't
Is, I know how to curse. The red plague rid you,
For learning me your language!

Newcomer Three   Brave monster!

Newcomer Four   Foolish more like . . . talking that way to a magician.

Newcomer Three   He might well be a slave, but his thoughts are free.

A leaf falls, the music plays.

Newcomer Three   Another message!

Newcomer Four   What does this one say?

Newcomer Three   'Nature's own shape of bud, bird, branch, or berry' – he's part of nature too!

Prospero
Hag-seed, hence!
Fetch us in fuel; and be quick, thou 'rt best,
To answer other business. Shrug'st thou, malice?
If thou neglect'st, or dost unwillingly
What I command, I'll rack thee with old cramps,
Fill all thy bones with aches, make thee roar,
That beasts shall tremble at thy din.

Caliban
No, pray thee.
(*Aside.*) I must obey. His art is of such power,

Prospero
So, slave, hence!

The story moves on.

Newcomer Three (*to the departing* **Prospero**)   You stole his home!

Newcomer Four   Wonder why that magican guy came here in the first place?

Newcomer Three   The names he called him – hag-seed, savage . . . slave.

Newcomer Four   We've been called worse. D'you think he was running away from something?

Beat.

Newcomer Three   Why's he so cruel?

Newcomer Four   'Cause he can be! There's no one to tell him to stop: a king with only one subject can say what he likes. Same here; same there. You know that!

Newcomer Three   I know that voice, that tone – those words . . . he's scared.

Newcomer Four   It's easy to see someone as a monster when you're scared.

Newcomer Three   We're not monsters are we?

Newcomer Four   No we're not.

The music again, more distant than before.

Newcomer Three   That strain again

Newcomer Four   Finds tongues in trees

The chapter ends as another begins . . .

Chapter Three

Unhappy Ending

A new chapter from The Taming of the Shrew *as another group emerges on stage, the townspeople, talking across the whole space, while* **Katherine** *sits, oblivious to them, until finally* **Petruchio** *steps from them to address her direct.* **Newcomers Five** *and* **Six** *watch on.*

Townsperson One   But who will marry her?

Townsperson Two   Katherine

Townsperson Three   Kate

Townsperson Four   Plain Kate

Townsperson Five   Katherine the curst

Townsperson One   So curst and shrewd

Townsperson Two   Intolerable curst

Townsperson Three   And shrewd and forward

Townsperson Four   An irksome, brawling scold

Townsperson Five   Famous for a scolding tongue

Townsperson One   That wench is stark mad

Townsperson Two   A most impatient devilish sprite

All   She's too rough for me!

Newcomer Five   She doesn't sound great.

Newcomer Six   They'd never say all that to her face.

Newcomer Five   Wanna bet? Looks like he's about to give it a try.

Petruchio
Good morrow, Kate, for that's your name, I hear.

Katherine
Well have you heard, but something hard of hearing.
They call me Katherine that do talk of me.

Petruchio
Hearing thy mildness praised in every town,
Thy virtues spoke of, and thy beauty sounded

Newcomer Six   He likes her!

Petruchio

Myself am moved to woo thee for my wife.

Newcomers Five *and* **Six**   Woah!

Katherine

'Moved,' in good time! Let him that moved you hither
Remove you hence.

Newcomers Five *and* **Six**   Roasted!

Petruchio

Come, come, you wasp! I' faith, you are too angry.

Katherine

If I be waspish, best beware my sting.

Petruchio

My remedy is then to pluck it out.

Katherine

Ay, if the fool could find it where it lies.

Petruchio

Who knows not where a wasp does wear his sting?
In his tail.

Katherine

In his tongue.

Petruchio

Whose tongue?

Katherine

Yours, if you talk of tales, and so farewell.

Petruchio

Nay, come again, good Kate. I am a gentleman –

Katherine

That I'll try.

She strikes him.

Petruchio
I swear I'll cuff you if you strike again.

Katherine
So may you lose your arms.

Petruchio
Nay, come, Kate, come. You must not look so sour.

Katherine
It is my fashion when I see a crab.

Petruchio
Why, here's no crab, and therefore look not sour.

Katherine
There is, there is.

Petruchio
Then show it me.

Katherine
Had I a glass, I would.

Petruchio
What, you mean my face?

Katherine
Well aimed of such a young one.

Petruchio
Now, by Saint George, I am too young for you.

Katherine
Yet you are withered.

Petruchio
'Tis with cares.

Katherine
I care not.

Petruchio
Nay, hear you, Kate – in sooth, you 'scape not so.

Katherine
I chafe you if I tarry. Let me go.

Petruchio
No, not a whit. I find you passing gentle.
O sland'rous world! Kate like the hazel twig
Is straight, and slender, and as brown in hue
As hazelnuts, and sweeter than the kernels.
O, let me see thee walk! Thou dost not halt.

Katherine
Go, fool, and whom thou keep'st command.

Newcomer Five   I don't care what people say about her,
she's brilliant!

Newcomer Six   And he really likes her, right?

Newcomer Five   She wouldn't touch him with a barge pole.

Newcomer Six   Stories always end up that way – they're
bound to get together.

Newcomer Five   When will you stop wishing life has fairy.
tale endings?

Newcomer Six   Nothing wrong with hoping . . .

Newcomer Five   Let it go.

As they say this we see **Petruchio** *slowly take her hand and lead her forward. The following text is spoken directly to the audience.*

Petruchio
Thus have I politicly begun my reign,
And 'tis my hope to end successfully.

Katherine
The more my wrong, the more his spite appears:
What, did he marry me to famish me?

Petruchio
She ate no meat to-day, nor none shall eat;
Last night she slept not, nor to-night she shall not;

Katherine
> Beggars, that come unto my father's door,
> Upon entreaty have a present alms;
> If not, elsewhere they meet with charity:

Petruchio
> As with the meat, some undeserved fault
> I'll find about the making of the bed;

Katherine
> But I, who never knew how to entreat,
> Nor never needed that I should entreat,

Petruchio
> And here I'll fling the pillow, there the bolster,
> This way the coverlet, another way the sheets:

Katherine
> Am starved for meat, giddy for lack of sleep,

Petruchio
> Ay, and amid this hurly I intend
> That all is done in reverend care of her;

Katherine
> With oaths kept waking and with brawling fed:

Petruchio
> And in conclusion she shall watch all night:

Katherine
> And that which spites me more than all these wants,
> He does it under name of perfect love;

Petruchio
> And if she chance to nod I'll rail and brawl
> And with the clamour keep her still awake.

Newcomer Five   He seemed nice before – but now, he's being a controlling –

Newcomer Six   They're playing games that's all.

Petruchio
This is a way to kill a wife with kindness;
And thus I'll curb her mad and headstrong humour.

Katherine
I prithee go and get me some repast;

Petruchio
He that knows better how to tame a shrew,

Katherine
I care not what, so it be wholesome food.

She is crouching or low by this point.

Petruchio
Now let him speak: 'tis charity to show.

The story moves on.

Newcomer Six   I told you they'd end up together.

Newcomer Five   Together? How is that together?

Newcomer Six   At least they have each other.

Newcomer Five   He has her. Tethered not together. That can't be her, it can't end like that!

Newcomer Six   Maybe he'll change.

Newcomer Five   She'll leave, won't she?

Another leaf lands as the snippet of music plays

Newcomer Six   Listen.

Newcomer Five   Look – another one . . . it says:
'Pine not
Rose up'

Newcomer Six   I think it's for her – Pine not, Rose up:
Rise up

Newcomer Five   For us all – let's change the ending.

Katherine *is surrounded by* **Newcomers Five** *and* **Six** *who say* '*Rise up! Rise up! Rise up!' to her. Other voices join in with this, and as the characters from* Twelfth Night *enter, they join in too, with a loud and buoyant energy until . . . this chapter closes and another starts.*

Chapter Four

A Joke Too Far

A new chapter from Twelfth Night *as* **Maria**, **Feste**, **Sir Toby** *and* **Sir Andrew** *pick up the 'Rise up!' chant making a rowdy racket.* **Malvolio** *enters – he is horrified at the noise and makes them the subject of his rage.* **Newcomers Seven** *and* **Eight** *watch on.*

Malvolio

My masters, are you mad? Or what are you? Have you no wit, manners, nor honesty, but to gabble like tinkers at this time of night? Do ye make an ale-house of my lady's house, that ye squeak out your coziers' catches without any mitigation or remorse of voice? Is there no respect of place, persons, nor time, in you?

Sir Toby

We did keep time, sir, in our catches. Sneck up!

Malvolio

Sir Toby, I must be round with you. My lady bade me tell you that, though she harbours you as her kins-man, she's nothing allied to your disorders. If you can separate yourself and your misdemeanours, you are welcome to the house; if not, and it would please you to take leave of her, she is very willing to bid you farewell.

Sir Toby, **Maria**, **Sir Andrew** *and* **Feste** *gather round him menacingly and tie him up, imprisoning him somewhere.*

Sir Toby, **Maria**, **Sir Andrew**, **Feste** *and* **All Ilyrians**
Rise up
O you are sick of self love

A kind of puritan
A time-pleaser;
An affectioned ass,
An overweening rogue,
How he jets under his advanced plumes
Go shake your ears
Out scab
Shall this fellow live?
Hang thee!
Why, we shall make him mad indeed

Newcomer Seven   Do you hear?

Newcomer Eight   What stuff is this?

Newcomer Seven   It is but trash.

Newcomer Eight   Trash talking that's for sure. Sounds like he winds them right up.

Newcomer Seven   But they've got him now . . .

Maria
Nay, I prithee, put on this gown and this beard; make him believe thou art Sir Topas the curate. Do it quickly.

Feste
Well, I'll put it on, and I will dissemble myself in't, and I would I were the first that ever dissembled in such a gown.

Sir Toby
Jove bless thee, Master Parson.

Feste
What ho, I say! Peace in this prison!

Sir Toby
The knave counterfeits well. A good knave.

Malvolio *within*.

Malvolio
Who calls there?

Feste

Sir Topas the curate, who comes to visit Malvolio the lunatic.

Malvolio

Sir Topas, Sir Topas, good Sir Topas, go to my lady.

Feste

Out, hyperbolical fiend! how vexest thou this man? Talkest thou nothing but of ladies?

Sir Toby

Well said, Master Parson.

Malvolio

Sir Topas, never was man thus wronged. Good Sir Topas, do not think I am mad. They have laid me here in hideous darkness.

Feste

Fie, thou dishonest Satan! I call thee by the most modest terms, for I am one of those gentle ones that will use the devil himself with courtesy. Say'st thou that house is dark?

Malvolio

As hell, Sir Topas.

Feste

Why, it hath bay windows transparent as barricadoes, and yet complainest thou of obstruction?

Malvolio

I am not mad, Sir Topas. I say to you this house is dark.

Feste

Madman, thou errest. I say there is no darkness but ignorance

Malvolio

I say this house is as dark as ignorance, though ignorance were as dark as hell; and I say there was never man thus abused. I am no more mad than you are.

Feste

Fare thee well.

Malvolio
  Sir Topas, Sir Topas!

Sir Toby
  My most exquisite Sir Topas!

Feste
  Nay, I am for all waters.

Maria
  Thou mightst have done this without thy beard and gown. He sees thee not.

Sir Toby
  To him in thine own voice, and bring me word how thou find'st him. I would we were well rid of this knavery. If he may be conveniently delivered, I would he were.

Exit.

Newcomer Seven   That's taking a joke too far.

Newcomer Eight   Maybe he deserved it – nothing more annoying than a pompous ass.

Newcomer Seven   You cram these words into my ears against the stomach of my sense.

Newcomer Eight   He's not the only preening fool around here.

Newcomer Seven   Hey! No one deserves that . . . it's terrible here, no better than what we left, we should never have come . . . I want to go HOME.

Newcomer Seven *looks upset – about to cry.* **Newcomer Eight** *is remorseful.*

Music and a leaf falls.

Newcomer Eight   Look – 'weep not green willow'. It's like the forest sees you – not like the others – really sees you: strong, young and sad, and is asking you to smile – or, you know, find tongues in trees.

Newcomer Seven   Books in the running brooks.

Newcomer Eight (*spoken up to the branches and trees above*)
Here shall he see no enemy

Newcomer Seven   But winter and rough weather

Newcomer Eight *puts their arms around* **Newcomer Seven** *as the story moves on . . .*

Chapter Five

A Reunion

A new chapter from The Comedy of Errors *begins as a new crowd of people fill the stage to create a busy marketplace.*

Antipholus/Crowd
 They say this town is full of cozenage;
 As, nimble jugglers that deceive the eye,
 Dark-working sorcerers that change the mind,
 Soul-killing witches that deform the body,
 Disguised cheaters, prating mountebanks,
 And many such-like liberties of sin:
 If it prove so, I will be gone the sooner

We see **Dromio of Syracuse** *and* **Dromio of Ephesus** *enter and move around the space; they are twins and they just miss each other as they pass.* **Dromio of Syracuse** *is furtive as he moves,* **Dromio of Ephesus** *more confident, looking for someone, maybe whistling.* **Newcomers Nine** *and* **Ten** *can move around the marketplace too; maybe each follows a different* **Dromio**.

The two **Dromios** *share the following text between them – in any way you wish – as they move.*

Dromios
 I to the world am like a drop of water
 That in the ocean seeks another drop;
 Who, failing there to find his fellow forth,
 Unseen, inquisitive, confounds himself:

Antipholus of Syracuse *steps out of the shadows, calls* **Dromio of Syracuse** *and hands over a bag of money.*

Antipholus of Syracuse
Dromio! Dromio! Dromio!
Go bear this to the Tavern, where we host,
And stay there, Dromio, till I come to thee.
Give out you are of this place
Lest that your goods too soon be confiscate.

Dromio of Syracuse *exits.*

Dromio of Ephesus *spots* **Antipholus of Syracuse** *and goes over to him.*

Antipholus of Syracuse
What now? How chance thou art return'd so soon?

Dromio of Ephesus
Return'd so soon! rather approach'd too late.
The capon burns, the pig falls from the spit;
The clock hath strucken twelve upon the bell –
My mistress made it one upon my cheek:
She is so hot because the meat is cold;
The meat is cold because you come not home –

Antipholus of Syracuse
Stop – in your wind, sir; tell me this, I pray:
Where have you left the money that I gave you?

Dromio of Ephesus
O, – sixpence that I had o'Wednesday last

Antipholus of Syracuse
Where is the gold I gave in charge to thee?

Dromio of Ephesus
To me, sir? why, you gave no gold to me!

Antipholus of Syracuse
Come tell me how thou hast dispos'd thy charge.

Dromio of Ephesus
  My charge was but to fetch you from the mart
  Home to your house, the Phoenix, sir, to dinner:
  My mistress and her sister stay for you.

Antipholus of Syracuse
  What mistress, slave, hast thou?

Dromio of Ephesus
  Your worship's wife, my mistress at the Phoenix;

Antipholus of Syracuse
  What, wilt thou flout me thus unto my face,
  Being forbid?

Strikes him.

Dromio of Ephesus
  What mean you, sir? for God's sake hold your hands!
  Nay, and you will not, sir, I'll take my heels.

Dromio of Ephesus *exits.*

Newcomer Nine   Direst cruelty.

Newcomer Ten   Relax. I don't think any of this is real. Only words –

Newcomer Nine   And beating!

Newcomer Ten   Oh come on it's not like anyone's been killed or anything.

Newcomer Nine   He called him a slave – treated him like one. Ignorant fools always talk with their fists too . . .

Antipholus of Syracuse
  The gold I gave to Dromio is laid up
  Safe at the tavern; here he comes again.

Dromio of Syracuse *enters.*

Antipholus of Syracuse
  How now, sir! is your merry humour alter'd?
  As you love strokes, so jest with me again.

You know no tavern? you receiv'd no gold?
Your mistress sent to have me home to dinner?

Dromio of Syracuse
When spake I such a word?

Antipholus of Syracuse
Even now, even here, not half-an-hour since.

Dromio of Syracuse
I did not see you since you sent me hence,
Home to the tavern with the gold you gave me.

Antipholus of Syracuse
Villain, thou didst deny the gold's receipt;
And told'st me of a mistress and a dinner;

Dromio of Syracuse
What means this jest? I pray you, master, tell me.

Antipholus of Syracuse
Yea, dost thou jeer and flout me in the teeth?
Think'st thou I jest? Hold, take thou that, and that.

Beats him.

Dromio of Syracuse
Hold, sir, for God's sake: now your jest is earnest:
Upon what bargain do you give it me?

Antipholus of Syracuse
If you will jest with me, know my aspect,
And fashion your demeanour to my looks,
Or I will beat this method in your sconce.

Dromio of Syracuse
I pray, sir, why am I beaten?

Antipholus of Syracuse
Dost thou not know?

Dromio of Syracuse
Nothing, sir, but that I am beaten.

Antipholus of Syracuse
Shall I tell you why?

Dromio of Syracuse
Ay, sir,

Antipholus of Syracuse
for flouting me;

Dromio of Syracuse
Was there ever any man thus beaten out of season,

Antipholus of Syracuse
Thou whoreson, senseless villain.

Dromio of Syracuse
I would I were senseless, sir, that I might not feel your blows.

Antipholus of Syracuse
Thou art sensible in nothing but blows, and so is an ass.

Antipholus of Syracuse *exits.*

Each **Dromio** *moves around the marketplace as they speak the following text, narrowly missing each other as they do, until they eventually discover each other.*

Dromio of Syracuse
I am an ass indeed; you may prove it by my long ears. I have served him from the hour of my nativity to this instant, and have nothing at his hands for my service but blows.

Dromio of Ephesus
When I am cold, he heats me with beating;

Dromio of Syracuse
when I am warm he cools me with beating.

Both
I am waked with it

Dromio of Ephesus
when I sleep, raised with it when I sit, driven out of doors with it when I go from home,

Dromio of Syracuse
welcomed home with it when I return.

Both
Nay –

Seeing each other they stop, look at each other. As they do so we hear the snippet of music and a leaf falls.

Newcomer Nine   Back together!

Newcomer Ten   As like as cherry is to cherry! I told you it wasn't all bad!

Newcomer Nine   It doesn't seem real.

Newcomer Ten   You have to keep believing. One day . . . you'll see.

Newcomer Nine   And another message from the forest – it says:

'Oak stout
Anchor bark'

Dromio of Ephesus
Methinks you are my glass, and not my brother:
I see by you I am a sweet-faced youth.

Dromio of Syracuse
Not I, sir; you are my elder.

Dromio of Ephesus
That's a question; how shall we try it?

Dromio of Syracuse
We'll draw cuts for the senior: till then, lead thou first.

Dromio of Ephesus
Nay, then, thus:
We came into the world like brother and brother:
And now let's go hand in hand, not one before another.

Newcomer Ten   Reunited – maybe that's what we needed to see! That everything works out in the end. Ok? So chill.

Newcomer Nine   But it's getting dark – and we are still here . . . it's almost night . . .

Newcomer Ten   'Oak stout anchor bark'

The story moves on . . .

Chapter Six

Murder Most Foul

A new chapter emerges from Macbeth. *Darkness falls but we have torches to light the way, as a group enter – it is hard to see their faces, who is who . . .*

Enter **Banquo**, *and* **Fleance**, *bearing a torch before him.*

Banquo
How goes the night, boy?

Fleance
The moon is down; I have not heard the clock.

Banquo
And she goes down at twelve.

Fleance
I take't, 'tis later, sir.

Banquo
Hold, take my sword. There's husbandry in Heaven,
Their candles are all out.
A heavy summons lies like lead upon me, And yet I would not sleep; merciful powers,
Restrain in me the cursed thoughts that nature
Gives way to in repose.

Macbeth *steps forward with his light.*

Banquo

Who's there?

He sees **Macbeth**.

Banquo

I dreamt last night of the three Weird Sisters;
To you they have showed some truth.

Macbeth

I think not of them:
Yet when we can entreat an hour to serve,
We would spend it in some words upon that business,
If you would grant the time.

Banquo

At your kind'st leisure.

Macbeth

If you shall cleave to my consent, when 'tis,
It shall make honour for you.

Banquo

So I lose none
In seeking to augment it, but still keep
My bosom franchised, and allegiance clear, I shall be
counselled.

Macbeth

Good repose the while.

Banquo

Thanks sir, the like to you.

Their faces are obscured and into the torchlight now comes the
Witches, *whisking up spells; they are going to cause trouble and
conjure the murderers.*

First Witch

Let us do mischief in the wood!

All Witches
Double, double, toil and trouble;
Fire burn and cauldron bubble

Newcomer Twelve   I don't like the sound of this at all.

Newcomer Eleven   Wicked!

Newcomer Twelve   This place gets darker and darker.

Newcomer Eleven   They're having fun though! Look!

First Witch
Thrice the brinded cat hath mew'd.

Second Witch
Thrice and once the hedge-pig whined.

Third Witch
Harpier cries, ''Tis time, 'tis time.'

Fourth Witch
Round about the cauldron go;
In the poison'd entrails throw.

Fifth Witch
Toad, that under cold stone
Days and nights has thirty-one
Swelter'd venom sleeping got,
Boil thou first i' the charmed pot.

All Witches
Double, double, toil and trouble;
Fire burn and cauldron bubble.

Second Witch
Fillet of a fenny snake,
In the cauldron boil and bake;

Third Witch
Eye of newt and toe of frog,
Wool of bat and tongue of dog,
Adder's fork and blind-worm's sting,
Lizard's leg and howlet's wing,

For a charm of powerful trouble,
Like a hell-broth boil and bubble.

All Witches
Double, double, toil and trouble;
Fire burn and cauldron bubble.

Fifth Witch
Scale of dragon, tooth of wolf,
Witch's mummy, maw and gulf
Of the ravin'd salt-sea shark,
Root of hemlock digg'd i' the dark,

Fourth Witch
Add thereto a tiger's chawdron,
For the ingredients of our cawdron.

Second Witch
Cool it with a baboon's blood,
Then the charm is firm and good.

First Witch
By the pricking of my thumbs,
Something wicked this way comes.

Newcomer Twelve   What have they done?

Newcomer Eleven   They've conjured up this lot . . . Wow!

The forest song is played but discordant and menacing.

Enter the **Murderers** *to the light as the* **Witches** *slip into the background to observe.*

First Murderer
But who did bid thee join with us?

Third Murderer
Macbeth.

Second Murderer
He needs not our mistrust; since he delivers
Our offices and what we have to do
To the direction just.

Fourth Murderer
Then stand with us.
The west yet glimmers with some streaks of day.
Now spurs the lated traveller apace,
To gain the timely inn; and near approaches
The subject of our watch.

Fifth Murderer
Hark! I hear horses.

Banquo (*stepping into the light once more*)
Give us a light there, ho!

Second Murderer
Then 'tis he; the rest
That are within the note of expectation
Already are i' th' court.

First Murderer
His horses go about.

Third Murderer
Almost a mile; but he does usually,
So all men do, from hence to the palace gate
Make it their walk.

We see **Banquo** *and* **Fleance** *with a torch.*

Fourth Murderer
A light, a light!

Fifth Murderer
'Tis he.

Sixth Murderer
Stand to't.

Banquo
It will be rain tonight.

All Murderers
Let it come down.

They kill **Banquo**.

Banquo
O, treachery! Fly, good Fleance, fly, fly, fly!

Dies. **Fleance** *escapes.*

Third Murderer
Who did strike out the light?

Sixth Murderer
Was't not the way?

Fifth Murderer
There's but one down: the son is fled.

Second Murderer
We have lost best half of our affair.

Fourth Murderer
Well, let's away, and say how much is done.

They fly off. The **Witches** *laugh in joy.*

Witches
The work is ill done!

They exit.

Newcomer Eleven   Murder. Now there's murder!

Music plays. A leaf falls.

Newcomer Twelve   Calm down – breathe – read what the
forest says.

Newcomer Eleven
'On a mountain-top the cedar shows,
That keeps his leaves in spite of any storm'

A gust and another leaf falls.

Newcomer Twelve   Oh and 'Summer comes though waves
billow'. It's telling us to be brave . . .

Newcomer Eleven   Bit late for that – I don't know if I can
keep going.

Newcomer Twelve   We need to. We always have. We always
do . . . come on. We must bear all. Together.

The story moves on . . .

Chapter Seven

The Ghost

A new chapter from Julius Caesar *as a procession enters; it's a
funeral.* **Caesar** *is laid out. People pass by respectfully paying their
condolences . . . Then* **Brutus** *stands up to speak.*

Brutus
Give me audience, friends.
Those that will hear me speak, let 'em stay here;
And public reasons shall be rendered
Of Caesar's death.

First Citizen
I will hear Brutus speak.

Second Citizen
The noble Brutus is ascended. Silence!

Brutus
Be patient till the last. Romans, countrymen, and lovers!
Hear me for my cause, and be silent, that you may hear.

If there be any in this assembly, any dear friend of
Caesar's, to him I say that Brutus' love to Caesar was no
less than his. If then that friend demand why Brutus rose
against Caesar, this is my answer: Not that I loved Caesar
less, but that I loved Rome more. Had you rather Caesar
were living and die all slaves, than that Caesar were dead
to live all freemen? As Caesar loved me, I weep for him; as
he was fortunate, I rejoice at it; as he was valiant, I honor
him; but as he was ambitious, I slew him. There is tears for
his love, joy for his fortune, honor for his valor, and death
for his ambition. Who is here so base that would be a
bondman? If any, speak, for him have I offended. Who is

here so rude that would not be a Roman? If any, speak, for him have I offended. Who is here so vile that will not love his country? If any, speak, for him have I offended. I pause for a reply.

The **Newcomers** *look around at the crowd and whisper to one another.*

Newcomer Thirteen   I mean it all makes sense what he says, but he's explaining why he killed someone . . . Are you okay with that? (*To the crowd.*) Is no one going to say anything!

Newcomer Fourteen   You think too much!

All   None, Brutus, none.

Brutus
Then none have I offended. I have done no more to Caesar than you shall do to Brutus. The question of his death is enrolled in the Capitol, his glory not extenuated, wherein he was worthy, nor his offenses enforced, for which he suffered death.

The crowd leave – some shake **Brutus**' *hand while others look unsure and whisper amongst themselves – they're not all buying* **Brutus**' *rhetoric . . .* **Brutus** *is left with his servants.*

Brutus
Farewell, everyone.

When they are all gone he turns to **Lucius**.

Brutus
Where is thy instrument?

Lucius
Here in the tent.

Brutus
What, thou speak'st drowsily?
Poor knave, I blame thee not, thou art o'er-watch'd.

Call Claudius and some other of my men;
I'll have them sleep on cushions in my tent.

Lucius
Varro and Claudius!

Enter **Varro** *and* **Claudius**.

Varro
Calls my lord?

Brutus
I pray you, sirs, lie in my tent and sleep;
(*To* **Lucius**.) Canst thou hold up thy heavy eyes awhile,
And touch thy instrument a strain or two?

Lucius
Ay, my lord, an't please you.

Brutus
It does, my boy.
I trouble thee too much, but thou art willing.

Lucius
It is my duty, sir.

Brutus
I should not urge thy duty past thy might;
I know young bloods look for a time of rest.

Lucius
I have slept, my lord, already.

Brutus
It was well done, and thou shalt sleep again;
I will not hold thee long. If I do live,
I will be good to thee.

Lucius *plays and sings till he falls asleep.*

Brutus
This is a sleepy tune. O murd'rous slumber,
Layest thou thy leaden mace upon my boy,
That plays thee music? Gentle knave, good night;

I will not do thee so much wrong to wake thee.
Let me see, let me see; is not the leaf turn'd down
Where I left reading? Here it is, I think.

Newcomer Thirteen   I don't like this. I've got a bad feeling
. . .

Newcomer Fourteen   It's suddenly so cold.

Enter the **Ghosts of Caesar** *– there can be as many or as few as
you like or even just one depending on preference; they don't all have
to speak or they could speak in unison at the discretion of the director.*

Brutus
Who comes here?
I think it is the weakness of mine eyes
That shapes this monstrous apparition.
Art thou some god, some angel, or some devil,
That mak'st my blood cold and my hair to stare?
Speak to me what thou art.

Ghosts
Thy evil spirit, Brutus.

Brutus
Why com'st thou?

Ghosts
To tell thee thou shalt see me again

Brutus
Well; then I shall see thee again?

Ghosts
Ay

Ghosts *vanish.*

Brutus
Now I have taken heart, thou vanishes.
Ill spirit, I would hold more talk with thee.
Boy! Lucius! Varro! Claudius! Sirs, awake! Claudius!

Lucius
The strings, my lord, are false.

Brutus
He thinks he still is at his instrument.
Lucius, awake!

Lucius
My lord?

Brutus
Didst thou dream, Lucius, that thou so criedst out?

Lucius
My lord, I do not know that I did cry.

Brutus
Yes, that thou didst. Didst thou see anything?

Lucius
Nothing, my lord.

Brutus
Sleep again, Lucius. Sirrah Claudius!
Fellow thou, awake!

Varro
My lord?

Claudius
My lord?

Brutus
Why did you so cry out, sirs, in your sleep?

Varro/Claudius
Did we, my lord?

Brutus
Ay. Saw you anything?

Varro
No, my lord, I saw nothing.

Claudius
    Nor I, my lord.

Brutus
    Go and commend me to my brother Cassius;
    Bid him set on his powers betimes before,
    And we will follow.

Varro/Claudius
    It shall be done, my lord.

The story moves on . . .

Newcomer Thirteen   We came here for sanctuary but the
woods are ruthless, dreadful, deaf and dull too – just like out
there.

Newcomer Fourteen   There are ghosts everywhere, at least
here we can sit alone, unseen of any.

Newcomer Thirteen   This is a shadowy desert, nothing for
us here.

Newcomer Fourteen   Bosky acres and unshrubbed down?
Midnight mushrooms, windring brooks and sedged crowns.

Newcomer Thirteen   But for how long? Exactly how long
will all that be here?

Music and another leaf.

Newcomer Fourteen   Look – listen. In nature's infinite
book of secrecy – a little we can read:

    'Under the cool shade of a sycamore
    Witness lofty cedars, grained ash, cloven pine,
    These moss trees that have outlived the eagle'

Newcomer Thirteen   That have outlived the eagle, and will
outlive us –

Newcomer Fourteen   It's saying the forest will always be
here . . . even when we're not.

Epilogue

Tongues in Trees

Taken from As You Like It *(and others).* Enter the **Heart of the Forest** *to the music we have heard throughout with all the Newcomers (except thirteen and fourteen) who are now united having experienced the stories of the forest.* **Newcomers Thirteen** *and* **Fourteen** *stand back and stare on in shock.*

Heart of the Forest
    Now, my co-mates and brothers in exile,
    Hath not old custom made this life more sweet
    Than that of painted pomp? Are not these woods
    More free from peril than the envious court?
    Here feel you not the penalty of Adam,
    The seasons' difference; as the icy fang
    And churlish chiding of the winter's wind,
    Which when it bites and blows upon your body,
    Even till you shrink with cold, you smile and say
    'This is no flattery; these are counsellors
    That feelingly persuade me what I am.'
    And this our life, exempt from public haunt,
    Finds tongues in trees, books in the running brooks,
    Sermons in stones, and good in everything.

Now the **Newcomers** *speak to the audience and to* **Newcomers Thirteen** *and* **Fourteen** *(unless there are only two* **Newcomers** *in which case the lines of* **Newcomers One–Twelve** *are spoken by the* **Heart of the Forest***).*

Newcomer One
    Do not these fair yokes
    Become the forest better than the town?

Newcomer Two
    Wherefore look'st thou sad
    When everything does make a gleeful boast?

Newcomer Three
   The birds chant melody on every bush;
   The snakes lie rolled in the cheerful sun;

Newcomer Four
   The green leaves quiver with the cooling wind
   And make a chequer'd shadow on the ground;

Newcomer Five
   Under their sweet shade, friends let us sit,

Newcomer Six
   And while the babbling echo mocks the hounds,
   Replying shrilly to the well-tun'd horns,

Newcomer Seven
   Let us sit down and mark their yellowing noise;

Newcomer Eight
   We may, each wreathed in the other's arms,

Newcomer Nine
   Our pastimes done, possess a golden slumber,

Newcomer Ten
   Whiles hounds and horns and sweet melodious birds

Newcomer Eleven
   Be unto us as is a nurse's song

Newcomer Twelve   Of lullaby to bring her babe asleep.

Newcomer Thirteen   I don't understand any of this – why
are they talking like that to us! Why are we seeing all this
– getting these notes – what's the point?

The **Newcomers** *take* **Newcomer Fourteen**'*s hand.*

Newcomer Fourteen
   Wait – My understanding
   Begins to swell, and the approaching tide
   Will shortly fill the reasonable shore

Newcomer Fourteen *holds out a hand to* **Newcomer Thirteen** *to join them all.*

Newcomer Thirteen   NO! I don't get it!

Another leaf with more words. **Newcomer Fourteen** *reads it.*

Newcomer Fourteen   'Place odes upon hawthorns and elegies on brambles.'

Newcomer Thirteen   Odes? Odes? Hold on – an ode is a song isn't it! It's a song.

They all join hands.

Newcomer Thirteen
Friendship makes us fresh.
And doth beget new courage in our breasts.

They all hold up the pieces of paper which are the lyrics of the song.

They all sing:

Place odes upon hawthorns and elegies on brambles
Under the cool shade of a sycamore
Witness lofty cedars, grained ash, cloven pine,
These moss trees that have outlived the eagle

Pine not
Rose up
Oak stout
anchor bark
weep not
green willow
Summer comes
Though waves billow

Nature's own shape of bud, bird, branch, or berry
Tell briers shall have leaves as well as thorns
As on a mountain-top the cedar shows,
That keeps his leaves in spite of any storm,

Pine not
Rose up
Oak stout
anchor bark
weep not
green willow
Summer comes
Though waves billow

Ends.

9 781350 440791